Hope
Notes
Devotions for Women
VOLUME 2

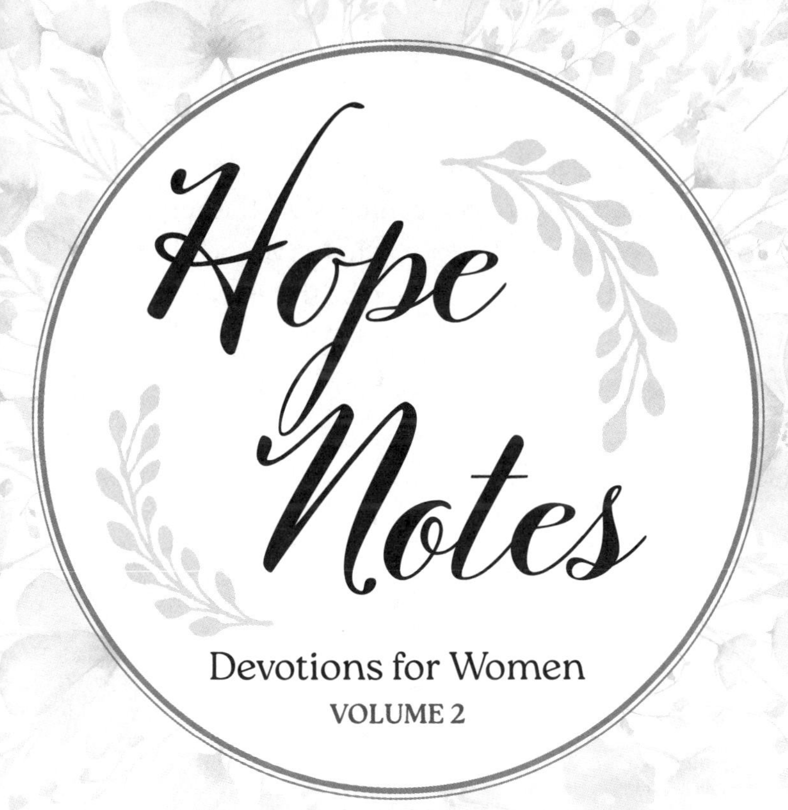

Hope Notes

Devotions for Women

VOLUME 2

Presidents of the Lutheran Women's Missionary League

Ida Mall, 1991–95

Gloria Edwards, 1995–99

Virginia Von Seggern, 1999–2003

Linda Reiser, 2003–7

Janice Wendorf, 2007–11

Kay Kreklau, 2011–15

Patti Ross, 2015–19

Debbie Larson, 2019–23

Eden Keefe, 2023–27

CONCORDIA PUBLISHING HOUSE · SAINT LOUIS

Dedicated to the memory of Betty Duda and to all the members of Lutheran Women in Mission, who serve the Lord with gladness. To God be the glory!

3558 S. Jefferson Ave., St. Louis, MO 63118-3968
1-800-325-3040 • cph.org

Manufactured in the United States of America

1 2 3 4 5 6 7 8 9 10 34 33 32 31 30 29 28 27 26 25

INTRODUCTION

During the 2020 COVID-19 pandemic, I started a project: writing out Bible verses about hope and promise on index cards. Sometimes I practiced simple calligraphy or fun lettering. Sometimes I used words cut from the pages of magazines or printed verses I found online. I added backgrounds of pretty paper or artwork from a grandson. It was fun being creative, but the point of recording the promise in this way was to slow down and enjoy the process—to reflect and focus on God's gifts.

In this book, you will find devotions and prayers by LWML presidents based on many of those "hope" verses. Our prayer is that when you get discouraged in our sinful world, you will be *en*couraged by God's Word and promises.

Eden Keefe, LWML president 2023–2027

The Lutheran Women's Missionary League (LWML) was established in 1942 as the official women's organization of The Lutheran Church—Missouri Synod. Today, as Lutheran Women in Mission, we honor that history and focus on affirming each woman's relationship with Christ, encouraging and equipping women to live out their Christian lives in active mission ministries, by serving their community at home, and by funding missions around the world with grants.

lwml.org

Ida
Mall

Life in the Blood

The blood of Jesus His Son cleanses us from all sin. (1 John 1:7)

Are you afraid of medical needles or blood? A male engineer friend who can fix almost anything is frightened at the sight of a needle or blood. He has fainted several times.

For Christians, blood covers sin. But not just any blood—the blood of Jesus Christ. Throughout the Old Testament, God directed His people to follow very specific ways of acquiring and using the blood of a one-year-old lamb to cover the sins of the people. During many years of trials and tribulations, through prophets and other means, God told His people that another special lamb would come.

Jesus, the Lamb, came to earth in human form. The baby Lamb's coming and purpose for coming are detailed in Matthew 1 and Luke 2. This Lamb was perfect. The giving of His one-time substitute blood for us on the cross covers and takes away our sins. Peter, the disciple who could not keep his promise to stay with Jesus when things got tough, wanted the world to know that his and our sins are forgiven not with silver or gold "but with the precious blood of Christ, like that of a lamb without blemish or spot" (1 Peter 1:19).

When we take Communion, we hear, "Take, eat; . . . take, drink; this is the true blood of our Lord and Savior Jesus Christ, shed for the forgiveness of your sins" (*LSB*, p. 199). Do these words have special meaning to you?

During surgery several years ago, I received four units of blood that helped save my earthly life. But it is the blood of Jesus that saves my life, my engineer friend's life, and your life—for eternity. True life is in the blood of Jesus. Amen.

Lord God, give me the steadfastness to count every hour as a gift from You. Strengthen my faith through Your Word today and grant peace to all in Your church. In Jesus' name. Amen.

Encouraging Words

Jesus said to him, "Feed My sheep." (John 21:17)

We never know when an encouraging or hopeful word is the medicine someone needs.

How can "feed My sheep" be encouraging words? Peter must have rejoiced to hear Jesus say these words. In the ongoing conversation recorded in John 21, Jesus asks Peter three times, "Do you love Me?" Each time, Peter's response is a positive yes. Peter must have realized that Jesus was forgiving him for denying three times that he was one of Jesus' disciples. With His words "feed My sheep," Jesus was entrusting forgiven Peter with proclaiming the message of salvation to the world. Jesus ends the conversation with the same two words used when they first met: "Follow Me" (Matthew 4:19).

God speaks encouraging words to us just as He spoke them to Peter. We read them in the Bible, from John 3:16, "For God so loved the world, that He gave His only son," to Joshua 1:9, "for the LORD your God is with you wherever you go," to Lamentations 3:22, "The steadfast love of the LORD never ceases; His mercies never come to an end."

God tells us in 1 Thessalonians 5:11 to "encourage one another and build one another up." How can we do that? a smile? pat on the back? brief note or text? phone call? greeting card? prayer? In the way that works for each of us, let us share Jesus with others. We are tasked only with sharing the love of Jesus with others. The other person's faith development is not our responsibility—that is the work of the Holy Spirit, who calls, gathers, enlightens, and sanctifies.

I literally used to feed sheep when I was young and lived on a farm. Today, am I concerned with figuratively feeding the sheep with encouraging words drawn from God's encouraging Word, the Bible. Let us pray:

> *Dear Father, remind and help us to use encouraging words to reflect Your everlasting love to others. In Jesus' name. Amen.*

Wait and Trust

> But as for me, I will look to the Lord; I will wait for the God of my salvation; my God will hear me. Rejoice not over me, O my enemy; when I fall, I shall rise; when I sit in darkness, the Lord will be a light to me. (Micah 7:7–8)

Is it difficult to wait for something? It is for most of us. If we have a problem, what is the first thing we do, try to solve it or pray and wait?

If we are facing bad times or problems that need fixing, we can read Micah 7. God sent the prophet Micah to confront the people of Judah and Samaria about their sins and the future of the two kingdoms. Micah told them they were "to do justice, and to love kindness, and to walk humbly with [their] God" (Micah 6:8). This message was totally dismissed, if it was heard at all. Micah says the people were evil and did evil very well. They did not trust one another, including their friends and neighbors. With members of families despising one another, Micah finishes chapter 7 highlighting the steadfast love of God and His compassion. These final words offered hope for a remnant of people who would return to God in the future. For now, though, Micah was going to wait and trust God to hear him and save him.

Years ago, a new electronic voting system was used at the national LWML convention in Kansas City. When the system failed, my patience was tested. As I stood at the podium, leading the meeting with thousands of women present, these words came from my lips: “If it doesn’t have anything to do with your salvation, don’t worry about it.” The words calmed the situation and reminded us why we were there—to serve the Lord. We waited, and eventually, the voting took place so we could carry on with our work.

Problems come. We can remember that our waiting for help is not in vain because the resolution we truly need has already been accomplished. Jesus solved the old problem of sin. And now, we await our never-ending forever with Jesus.

Dear Lord, help us wait, trust, and be ready to tell others about the God of our salvation. Amen.

Joyful Face

A glad heart makes a cheerful face, but by sorrow of heart the spirit is crushed. (Proverbs 15:13)

Trinity Lutheran School had its final school day, after sixty-seven years of serving the Baton Rouge community (and our two children, in its early days). I attended the closing service and knew immediately that my one facial tissue would not be enough. Just then, I looked ahead to my left and saw a kindergartner standing and singing with such joy and gusto that my sadness was quelled. I just had to smile. During the singing, the child turned and saw me. Together, from a distance, we did the motions of not letting that light of Jesus be hidden under a bushel basket. We were going to let it shine!

When asked what their theme word for that year had been, the children readily responded, "*Connected*," as in the vine and the branches. The closing program was designed to help the students remember they are God's children, to remain connected to Jesus, and to share the love of Jesus with those they would meet in their new schools.

As we live each day with joy, and with sadness at times, let us remember that the Holy Spirit is always working in us to keep us connected to the power of God.

As a branch of the Vine, let us produce the fruit of the Spirit—love, joy, peace, patience, kindness, goodness, faithfulness, gentleness, and self-control.

The closing of the school started as a day of sadness, but it became a day of joy because one little boy let the light of Jesus fill his face and shine outward. Just as Jesus intends us all to do!

Dear Father, thank You for being with us in the good and the sad times. Help us to have joyful faces that reflect Your love. In the name of Jesus. Amen.

Normal Day

Fully convinced that God was able to do what He had promised. (Romans 4:21)

It was a normal October day when I had my yearly mammogram. A Friday in 1995. What could go wrong?

Many X-rays later, I sat by myself in a small room. Some relief came from a Mustard Seed devotional packet that was in my purse. I chose one at random. The Bible verse and devotion reminded me that God kept His promises to Abraham. With no cell phone of today and no Bible with me, I was unable to look up the verse to read the context.

I went home that day with the instruction to see my doctor again on Monday. Over the weekend, God prepared my heart and mind through His Word. As I read and studied Romans 4, especially verses 13–25, I was reminded to have faith and to trust God. At the end of Romans 4, God says that Abraham's faith was counted as righteousness. Yes, God keeps His promises.

That Monday morning my doctor told me I had breast cancer. I know you will understand that it was not a happy day. It was a day to trust God. To be assured that He was with me, no matter what. At that time I coined my saying, "I'm always going home, to my earthly home or to my heavenly home."

The last verses of Romans 4 assure us that God counts us righteous by faith in Jesus, who was crucified and died. By that death, He paid the price for our sins. Through our Savior, we have sure hope for now and all eternity.

Consider thinking about God's promises to you by reading Romans 4:13–25.

Dear Jesus, help me to trust that You are with me through the trials of this world. May each day be a normal day of trusting Your promises. Amen.

Gloria
Edwards

Hope Brings Boldness

Since we have such a hope, we are very bold. . . . Now the Lord is the Spirit, and where the Spirit of the Lord is, there is freedom. And we all, with unveiled face, beholding the glory of the Lord, are being transformed into the same image from one degree of glory to another. For this comes from the Lord who is the Spirit. (2 Corinthians 3:12, 17–18)

Think of your past, recent or long past. Can you remember moments that you wish you could take back? Perhaps you said or did something that was inappropriate. You are certainly forgiven. Were there moments when you were not bold? When you wish that you had injected a comment or two about your faith or given testimony to your life in our Lord?

It's not always easy to be bold. However, since we have hope in Jesus, our Lord and Savior, we can overcome shyness and reticence. That hope gives us the freedom to be bold—always. As we strive to emulate our Lord, we can trust in Him for His help and guidance.

Look for opportunities to share your faith, to share your freedom because of the hope that you have in your heart. Build relationships, because then it becomes more fruitful to share. Chat with your neighbor. Invite friends for coffee and conversation. Care about those you know. Then, be bold in sharing the hope that lives in your heart.

Dear Jesus, we come to You knowing that You are our Lord, our Savior. Help us build relationships with neighbors and others we know. We ask that You give us boldness as we share our hope in You. We ask because we know that You want all to come to You. Bless us and keep us safe. Amen.

We Rest in God Alone

> For God alone my soul waits in silence; from Him comes my salvation. He alone is my rock and my salvation, my fortress; I shall not be greatly shaken. . . . For God alone, O my soul, wait in silence, for my hope is from Him. He only is my rock and my salvation, my fortress; I shall not be shaken. On God rests my salvation and my glory; my mighty rock, my refuge is God. Trust in Him at all times, O people; pour out your heart before Him; God is a refuge for us. (Psalm 62:1–2, 5–8)

Troubles are everywhere. Troubles in the news. Troubles around the world. Divisiveness in the nation. Unrest in the family. Arguments and strife. When chaos is all around us, where do we turn for peace? It often seems impossible to find comfort and assurance.

King David was definitely troubled. He was threatened on many sides. So where did he turn? He turned to God, his rock and refuge. His hope for lasting peace was in God alone. And we know that God answered his plea.

We all need peace. We all need the comfort of knowing that we can put all our trust in our God. As you lay down to rest, pray that your soul will find what it needs. Let the words of the psalm encourage you to trust God and the hope that comes through Him. Allow Him to be your rock and your refuge! Then we will not be shaken!

Dear Lord, in these times of trouble and turmoil, grant us peace in the hope that You are our rock and refuge. Help us put our trust in You always. We ask in the name of Jesus, our Lord and Savior. Amen.

Hold Fast to Your Hope

For whatever was written in former days was written for our instruction, that through endurance and through the encouragement of the Scriptures we might have hope. May the God of endurance and encouragement grant you to live in such harmony with one another, in accord with Christ Jesus, that together you may with one voice glorify the God and Father of our Lord Jesus Christ. (Romans 15:4–6)

What's your answer to this question: Is it fruitful to spend time in the Word of God? After all, those words were written so many years ago. Could they have any relevance to our busy lives today?

For those of us who follow Jesus, the answer is easy. Of course we can learn from the Scriptures. We find encouragement in the hope that we have in Jesus. This is not always easy in the face of questions and sometimes arrogant comments. Our busy lives can get in the way of reading and learning and studying Scripture.

But we must continue to earnestly study what the Bible tells us. The apostle Paul, who came to know Jesus later in life, was a lifetime learner. He never stopped, and he encourages us to be unified in the hope that we have in our salvation. In every circumstance, we know we can trust in our Jesus. Through Him, we glorify God as we share our complete trust in the hope we have in His grace and peace for us. That sharing is not always easy, but the Holy Spirit will give you the words of encouragement when you need them.

Set aside quality time to study and meditate on Scripture. It helps to use study guides or a study Bible. Commit to learn and share your learning today. And know that God's Word speaks to you in special ways in all circumstances. Every word there was written to give you hope.

Dear Jesus, we ask that You give us the will to commit to continual learning. Help us set aside a time and place to study and talk with You. Help us hold fast to the hope we have in You and our salvation. In Your holy name. Amen.

His Mercy Gives Hope

> But when the goodness and loving kindness of God our Savior appeared, He saved us, not because of works done by us in righteousness, but according to His own mercy, by the washing of regeneration and renewal of the Holy Spirit, whom He poured out on us richly through Jesus Christ our Savior, so that being justified by His grace we might become heirs according to the hope of eternal life. (Titus 3:4–7)

Oh, mercy! Mercy me! Have mercy! Those words were spoken by my dear, wonderful grandmother. They came especially when there was some stress; perhaps when she was putting a pie in the oven or getting the meal to the table as soon as the hungry farmworkers sat down. Somehow, she almost always completed those tasks very well and on time.

Just what does *mercy* mean, anyway? One way to define it is "unmerited compassion or love." Something that is not deserved or earned in any way. When it comes to our lives as Christians, not one of us deserves the love, blessings, mercy, and grace that Jesus gives us freely and completely. When we take a moment to think about our flaws and frailties, it's quite depressing to dwell on what we each deserve. The truth is that you and I earn nothing but punishment. We do not deserve the free forgiveness we have. We can do nothing to earn forgiveness and nothing to earn eternal life.

It is also true that we have God's mercy. We have His love. We are His dear children, made His by the work of the Holy Spirit in the Word and water of Baptism. Therefore, we are His heirs, and we have the hope, the certainty, of eternal life. What an incredible blessing!

Dear Father in heaven, we give our thanks to You for the gift of Your Son, Jesus, our Lord and Savior. It is through His death and resurrection that we, through unlimited mercy, have the hope and the promised gift of eternal life. We ask this in the name of Jesus. Amen.

Faith Gives Us Hope

> Let us draw near with a true heart in full assurance of faith, with our hearts sprinkled clean from an evil conscience and our bodies washed with pure water. Let us hold fast the confession of our hope without wavering, for He who promised is faithful. (Hebrews 10:22–23)

I remember some of the teachings in my small Lutheran grade school many years ago. One of those asked, *What does faith mean?*

Our teacher had a chair in front of the class and asked if we thought it would hold if we sat on it. Did we believe it would? When we all said yes, he responded that we believed the chair was strong and durable, which meant that we had faith in its ability to hold us. We had *faith*!

That was a simple demonstration for young children. How does that understanding relate to our faith as adults? The same sort of proof is evident everywhere. Every day, God demonstrates His care and concern for each of us. The world turns, and the sun shines. We live and breathe. We are surrounded by others to care for and who care for us. Most important, we have the promises of our God. These promises, revealed to us in His Word, teach us about the sacrifice of His Son, Jesus, on our behalf. The Holy Spirit gives us faith to know that

God's Word is true. We can trust in the hope in Jesus that we profess.

It's not always easy to hold on to our faith. Trouble and fear can try to take away the peace we long for. The sin-darkened world wants us to question our understanding of Scripture. But we can rely on the faith we were given in Baptism. His promises are true!

Dear Jesus, we thank You for Your faithful care for each of us. We know we have forgiveness through Your great sacrifice. Help us cling to that belief. Strengthen our faith so that our hope in You is lasting. Amen.

Virginia
Von
Seggern

Filled with Hope

And now, O Lord, for what do I wait? My hope is in You. (Psalm 39:7)

Here I am again—writing about hope in Jesus. I've been here before. When the first *Hope Notes* was published, I contributed a few things that (I hope) reminded readers about the source of our hope: Jesus, who promises us forgiveness and heaven with Him. But that wasn't the first time I was called to write about hope. More than twenty-five years ago, I was tasked with writing devotions about the hope we have in our Savior for people throughout the state of Nebraska. This assignment was part of a campaign to support a program called Share the Hope, with Lutheran Family Services of Nebraska. The years-long project included very large celebrations held throughout the state and featured well-known speakers like Betty Duda and Rev. Dr. Oswald Hoffmann. And it was successful, raising millions of dollars for the work of the organization, which included disaster response, aid to families, and support for refugees (among other projects).

Through this campaign, the sweet sound of hope was spread by faithful pastors and outstanding speakers. Everyone was filled with songs and sounds of hope in the promise of Jesus Christ. Being part of it was such a fulfilling job, one that required many hours of work and many miles of traveling and meeting interesting people. One of those people was Shirley, who belonged to a different church body. She and I discussed many topics, terms, and theological tenets as we found common ground in God's Word. We also found lasting friendship.

Why is this story important to you today? It's because that same hope is yours right now. In whatever work you do, you are tasked with sharing the hope you have in Jesus. You are equipped for this task by the Holy Spirit, who gives you faith to believe in Jesus and who gives you the words to talk about Him. Your work might not raise millions of dollars, but it will do this one thing: fill you with hope. I am definitely overflowing with this hope!

My hope is built on nothing less
Than Jesus' blood and righteousness;
No merit of my own I claim
But wholly lean on Jesus' name.
On Christ, the solid rock, I stand;
All other ground is sinking sand,
All other ground is sinking sand. (*LSB* 576:1)

Hope That Lasts a Lifetime

Why are you cast down, O my soul, and why are you in turmoil within me? Hope in God; for I shall again praise Him, my salvation and my God. (Psalm 42:11)

I have hope in God. It has been in me for as long as I can remember—all during my childhood, during my growing years, and today. My parents were wonderful Christians who joined a Lutheran congregation on my second birthday. That was when we all were baptized. That was when God planted hope in my heart.

An inspiration and example of service for me was my mom. She belonged to Women's Circle, or Ladies' Aid, and took her turn volunteering for various jobs within the church. My dad also volunteered for many jobs. Whatever needed to be done, they worked with others to do it. We spent time at church worshiping, singing in choir, helping with soup suppers and bazaars. If the door was open for a church activity, we were there.

I still remember the little white-frame church across the street from the school I attended. I was confirmed in that church, after attending the usual confirmation classes. By helping with VBS, singing in the choir, playing the organ, teaching Sunday school, and serving with the youth group, I was constantly engaged with learning, helping, and growing in faith. And I still am! I've never known a time that I didn't hope in Jesus Christ.

The story of your life of faith might be similar to mine. Or it might be very different. Maybe you came to faith as an adult. Maybe you are the only Christian in your family. Or maybe you have a family Bible that records births and Baptisms for generations.

Whatever path your journey has taken, and whatever rocky trails you have traveled, you can thank God that the hope in Jesus that is yours through faith sustains you every day of your life—on this day and forever.

When darkness veils His lovely face,
I rest on His unchanging grace;
In ev'ry high and stormy gale
My anchor holds within the veil.
On Christ, the solid rock, I stand;
All other ground is sinking sand,
All other ground is sinking sand. (*LSB* 576:2)

Heavenly Peace

Send out Your light and Your truth; let them lead me; let them bring me to Your holy hill and to Your dwelling! Then I will go to the altar of God, to God my exceeding joy, and I will praise You with the lyre, O God, my God. Why are you cast down, O my soul, and why are you in turmoil within me? Hope in God; for I shall again praise Him, my salvation and my God. (Psalm 43:3–5)

One of my favorite memories is the Christmas after our daughter died. That such a sad milestone is a favorite memory for me may seem strange, but it marked a special event in our family. Everyone was home: her brother and sister, their families, and her two children. Naturally, we were a little awkward, and we wondered how to celebrate that first year in a way that didn't bring any more sorrow. I was determined that we would not do anything the same way as we did before. So we went outside our regular routine—and went outside.

We went Christmas caroling, visiting all the neighbors on nearby farms. We piled in and out of cars and pickups. We praised God with our voices, and it was beautiful! The singers in our family are strong and can hold a tune without accompaniment. Sopranos, altos, tenors, and basses blended in perfect harmony to bring joy, comfort, and heavenly peace as we celebrated our hope in our Savior. And we made everyone in our family and those we visited happy and fulfilled in the hope in the resurrection that we share.

Our mission to do something different that year was accomplished. And it meant something extra special for us, because even as we mourned our daughter's death, we were thankful that through Jesus, she is worshiping at His heavenly throne. Praise the Lord!

His oath, His covenant and blood
Support me in the raging flood;
When ev'ry earthly prop gives way,
He then is all my hope and stay.
On Christ, the solid rock, I stand;
All other ground is sinking sand,
All other ground is sinking sand. (*LSB* 576:3)

Plans for the Future

Not only that, but we rejoice in our sufferings, knowing that suffering produces endurance, and endurance produces character, and character produces hope, and hope does not put us to shame, because God's love has been poured into our hearts through the Holy Spirit who has been given to us. (Romans 5:3–5)

I'm a widow, and the years I've spent by myself on the farm have been quiet, occasionally lonely, busy, and sometimes difficult. I'm independent, but once in a while, I have to ask for help from Jim and Phyllis, my closest neighbors. This usually involves repairing something or putting something together.

I've always wanted to stay here on the farm. I can easily get to where I want to go, and, besides, I own the property. That makes things easier. But there is a little voice of doubt speaking in my ear, asking if I want to retire, downsize, and move to town. Then my family weighs in, one with one idea and another with a different option. All this adds to the position I'm in as I mull things over, pray, and plan.

I've always been sure that God has plans for me. "For I know the plans I have for you, declares the LORD, plans for welfare and not for evil, to give you a future and a hope" (Jeremiah 29:11).

What did I decide about my plans? Nothing. I'm still on the farm by myself and still enjoy it. The neighbors still help when I need it. And that voice in my ear still raises doubts. My plans about my living arrangements may change at a moment's notice, but the Lord's plans for my future are very clear: My eternal home is with Him.

> Let not your hearts be troubled. Believe in God; believe also in Me. In My Father's house are many rooms. If it were not so, would I have told you that I go to prepare a place for you? And if I go and prepare a place for you, I will come again and will take you to Myself, that where I am you may be also. And you know the way to where I am going. (John 14:1–4)

His oath, His covenant and blood
Support me in the raging flood;
When ev'ry earthly prop gives way,
He then is all my hope and stay.
On Christ, the solid rock, I stand;
All other ground is sinking sand,
All other ground is sinking sand. (*LSB* 576:3)

Wait, with Patience

And not only the creation, but we ourselves, who have the first fruits of the Spirit, groan inwardly as we wait eagerly for adoption as sons, the redemption of our bodies. For in this hope we were saved. Now hope that is seen is not hope. For who hopes for what he sees? But if we hope for what we do not see, we wait for it with patience. (Romans 8:23–25)

Hope for something we can't see? Waiting with patience for it?

In my profession of nursing, I learned that when you have a problem, you don't wait. You fix it—NOW. Not two hours from now. Someone's life might depend on it. That tendency followed me through my entire life; whatever the problem, I work to fix it.

But as I get older, I have started to defer thinking about the current problem, wait for someone to come along with help, and do something else. I'm not so acutely tempted to fix the problem at hand. Perhaps I've developed more patience? More likely, it's that the nature of the problems has changed, since I'm not in job-related life-or-death situations anymore.

There's one problem I've never been able to fix—how to deal with sin and death. Can I fix my sin? No. Can I do anything about death? No.

So what can I do? Wait. With patience. Wait with confident faith that Jesus has fixed the problem of sin and has made eternal life possible. Wait with patient hope for heaven, the resurrection, seeing God face to face, asking Paul a few questions. These things will come to fruition soon enough; only God knows the timing. I'm satisfied with that.

When He shall come with trumpet sound,
Oh, may I then in Him be found,
Clothed in His righteousness alone,
Redeemed to stand before His throne!
On Christ, the solid rock, I stand;
All other ground is sinking sand,
All other ground is sinking sand. (*LSB* 576:4)

Linda
Reiser

Household of Faith

> Remembering before our God and Father your work of faith and labor of love and steadfastness of hope in our Lord Jesus Christ. (1 Thessalonians 1:3)

What does a household of faith look like? I am beyond grateful to my parents and extended family to have been grounded in my faith as a child. What does that look like? For me, it was daily prayers; it was attending Sunday school and church regularly; it was serving our neighbors and community. This verse reminds me our foundation of faith includes love and hope.

Faith is active, not passive. From the acts of kindness to the moments spent in prayer, these reflect faith in action. He equips us for every good work He has prepared for us.

Love is the foundation of all we do, from caring for our families to serving others in our community. That love mirrors God's love for us. Through the love we give to others, we reflect the perfect love Jesus gives us. That has a profound impact—on us and on them.

Hope in Jesus Christ anchors us despite our uncertain and challenging world. Hope gives us the strength to endure trials and hardships and to remain steadfast in our faith. We have confidence that our struggles are temporary and that a glorious future awaits.

Take a moment today to thank God for His faithfulness in allowing you to live out your faith, love, and hope to others. Thank Him for showing perfect love for you in Jesus. Ask Him to continue to strengthen your faith, deepen your love, and renew your hope each day.

Come, Thou Fount of ev'ry blessing,
Tune my heart to sing Thy grace;
Streams of mercy, never ceasing,
Call for songs of loudest praise.
While the hope of endless glory
Fills my heart with joy and love,
Teach me ever to adore Thee;
May I still Thy goodness prove. (*LSB* 686:1)

Finding Strength in God

Have you not known? Have you not heard? The LORD is the everlasting God, the Creator of the ends of the earth. He does not faint or grow weary; His understanding is unsearchable. He gives power to the faint, and to him who has no might He increases strength. Even youths shall faint and be weary, and young men shall fall exhausted; but they who wait for the LORD shall renew their strength; they shall mount up with wings like eagles; they shall run and not be weary; they shall walk and not faint. (Isaiah 40:28–31)

Do the demands of the day, work, family, activities, church, and relationships ever exhaust you? Maybe you are weighed down by responsibilities and the uncertainty of the future. In those moments of life, these verses from Isaiah bring us comfort and strength.

The comfort from these timeless words of Isaiah has helped me serve two of my neighbors. Both women have lost their husbands, sooner than anticipated and unexpectedly. Both have wondered how they can manage, and they feel overwhelmed. These Isaiah verses have been a blessing and an opportunity to share with them that God is unfailing in His strength and understanding. He is everlasting. He does not grow tired or weary like we do. Even in our weakness, He provides the strength we need.

Although their circumstances have not changed, God has given them hope and strength to face each day with courage and grace. As we all face uncertainties and exhaustion in our daily lives, our strength comes from the Lord. As we place our hope in Him, He will renew our strength, enabling us to run the race set before us with endurance, hope, and joy!

Heavenly Father, help us to trust in You completely. May we soar on wings like eagles, reflecting Your glory in all we do. In Jesus' name. Amen.

Don't Let Go

Behold, the eye of the Lord is on those who fear Him, on those who hope in His steadfast love. . . . Our soul waits for the Lord; He is our help and our shield. For our heart is glad in Him, because we trust in His holy name. Let Your steadfast love, O Lord, be upon us, even as we hope in You. (Psalm 33:18, 20–22)

Many good things are lost by sheer neglect or lack of perseverance. For an illustration, imagine holding a plate by two fingers, then letting it drop. It would shatter when it hits the floor. You didn't really break that plate; you just let the plate go, and it broke itself. So it is with many things we experience in life—our relationships, our character, and even our faith. We quickly lose them if we neglect them and let them go.

We are reminded in Psalm 33 to put our hope in God's unfailing love. Hope and prayer link us with the loving, living Lord and keep us from letting go.

Hope is different than wishing things were different; hope is a confident expectation. It is confidence in God's love, wisdom, and power. It is faith that His Word is true, especially the part about Jesus coming with promise and peace because He loves us so much that He gave His life to pay for our wrongs.

Hope is hanging on, not letting go of the certainty that the Lord sees, knows, loves, forgives, and saves us. His plans for our future are good and filled with hope, even when we cannot understand.

Heavenly Father, thank You for Your unfailing love and faithfulness toward us. Help us to place our hope in You alone. May Your love surround us and fill our hearts with joy and peace. In Jesus' name. Amen.

Heart Renewal

So we do not lose heart. Though our outer self is wasting away, our inner self is being renewed day by day. For this light momentary affliction is preparing for us an eternal weight of glory beyond all comparison, as we look not to the things that are seen but to the things that are unseen. For the things that are seen are transient, but the things that are unseen are eternal. (2 Corinthians 4:16–18)

Is it a difficult health diagnosis? Is it a serious illness? Is it a family member who has chosen a different lifestyle? Is it the reality of aging and making decisions that are difficult but needed? It does not take much for our world to be turned upside down. We may begin to struggle when the daily challenges of life and the weight of these worries seem overwhelming.

Look again at 2 Corinthians 4:16: "So we do not lose heart. Though our outer self is wasting away, our inner self is being renewed day by day." Jesus saw everything and everyone as being alive and full of possibilities. Our struggles are real and painful, but they are temporary. That's because each of us is promised an eternal glory through our faith in Jesus' sacrifice for us. Those trials today shape our character and deepen our faith in ways we cannot see.

This gives us a renewed sense of hope. Those worries that overwhelm and exhaust us in our daily lives suddenly, with God's promise, produce comfort and renew our hearts to know nothing we experience today compares to the glory He promises for each one of us.

How can you be inspired to fix your eyes on Jesus and find strength and hope in Him for His eternal promises? As you think through your answer to this question, discuss it with a friend, or write about it in your journal, let your response guide your prayers.

Heavenly Father, thank You for giving me all I need today to love and serve You according to Your will for me. Thank You, especially, for the promise and hope I have in Jesus. In His name. Amen.

Get Ready, Get Set, Go!

But in your hearts honor Christ the Lord as holy, always being prepared to make a defense to anyone who asks you for a reason for the hope that is in you; yet do it with gentleness and respect. (1 Peter 3:15)

How many times have you started a children's race with "Get ready, get set, go!" Everyone begins running as fast and hard as they can. It is your countdown, your voice, and your signal that starts the race in motion.

In 1 Peter 3:15, the Lord reminds us how we can get ready, get set, and go!

Get ready: Be prepared with the knowledge and understanding of our hope in Christ through hearing the Word and Bible study.

Get set: We are encouraged to give an answer "with gentleness and respect." What does that mean? As challenging as it can be to share our hope with some family or friends, we are called to not yell or sell but to tell about Jesus with a humble attitude.

Go: Be ready to defend our hope in Christ. Why are you a Christian? someone might ask. We can answer with confidence that we are broken because of our sin, but we have God's grace and Christ's sacrifice and love and the assurance of eternal life in heaven. That is our defense; it is the distinction in each of us that is different from the world. Bible study, worship, and Christian fellowship are meant not only for us to internalize and learn but also to prepare us to go out and tell about Jesus.

> My hope is built on nothing less
> Than Jesus' blood and righteousness;
> No merit of my own I claim
> But wholly lean on Jesus' name. (*LSB* 576:1)

Janice
Wendorf

Know the Hope!

> Having the eyes of your hearts enlightened, that you may know what is the hope to which He has called you, what are the riches of His glorious inheritance in the saints. (Ephesians 1:18)

What do you know? As I thought about this question, I easily came up with several things I know, including my name, address, telephone number, and Social Security number; names and ages of family members and friends; my growing list of medical personnel; the fact that Jesus loves me; and many hymns, prayers, and creeds—all important things to know. And that is just scratching the surface.

As a former English teacher, I couldn't help but notice that Ephesians 1:15–21 is all one sentence in the ESV translation. Nestled in the middle of this is verse 18, and the middle of verse 18 is "that you may know what is the hope to which He has called you."

What is it that Paul wants them to know? Paul's desire and prayer for the Ephesians is that they may know that God, Himself, has called them. We, as His called people, have the riches of His glorious inheritance in the saints.

We also have His numerous promises. Psalm 103:12 assures us, "As far as the east is from the west, so far does He remove our transgressions from us." Total forgiveness. Jesus told us in John 14:2–3 that He is going to prepare a place for us, and He will come again to take us to be with Him. God's promises are in His Word. Look for them and believe them.

Read Ephesians 1:15–23. God's love for us comes through loud and clear, and it contains a wealth of prayer prompts.

Back to my list in the first paragraph, the most important thing I know is the hope I have in Christ Jesus!

Dear Jesus, thank You for Your faithfulness and goodness to me, for being my source of strength and hope. Thank You for the promise of an eternal inheritance with You. Amen.

Continual Hope

> But I will hope continually and will praise You yet more and more. My mouth will tell of Your righteous acts, of Your deeds of salvation all the day, for their number is past my knowledge. (Psalm 71:14–15)

"But I will hope continually." How is that working for you? Continual hope? Personally, I struggle with this, tending to focus on the negative. When I find myself mired in melancholy, these words of Psalm 71 remind me where my focus should be.

The psalmist looks to the righteous acts of God and the deeds of salvation. The righteous acts of God include His saving grace, love, mercy, justice, and faithfulness to His covenants and promises. God's deeds of salvation are seen in the birth, life, death, resurrection, and ascension of Jesus Christ, securing life eternal for all who believe in Him.

Two other things impressed me. The first is "my mouth will tell." The psalmist leaves no wiggle room here. Hope leads to praise, and praise leads to telling. God has given me lips to tell what He has done for me.

For the second thing, notice what he says in the last phrase: "for their number is past my knowledge." You and I will never fully grasp and know all of God's righteous acts and His deeds of salvation. What a mighty God we serve!

The notes for Psalm 71:14–15 in *The Lutheran Study Bible* read, "[The] Psalmist's life of faith and hope will show itself in witness and praise" (*TLSB*, p. 915). The psalmist focuses on God's righteous acts. He is filled with hope. In a sense, he became historical, remembering what God has done and continues to do. And that will work well for us too.

O God, You are "our help in ages past" and "our hope for years to come" (LSB *733:1). I praise and thank You. In Jesus' name. Amen.*

Set Your Hope

> Therefore, preparing your minds for action, and being sober-minded, set your hope fully on the grace that will be brought to you at the revelation of Jesus Christ. (1 Peter 1:13)

When I watch athletic contests like the Olympics, I'm impressed with the amount of preparation, intentional focus, and discipline the athletes demonstrate. Many of them train for years honing their skills. For some individuals it may be for just one race, jump, swim, or routine.

How long have you been preparing for your personal Olympics?

In the text, the apostle Peter is encouraging his readers to prepare their minds for action. When will you be put to the test? It may be a tragedy that comes into your life—health issues, cancer, aging, impending death of a loved one, or your own death.

Peter instructs readers to be sober-minded, to live with a single focus, living with eternity in view. It's the conscious decision to acknowledge God's truth and His wisdom above our own, to rely not on ourselves but on His wisdom alone.

Our confidence comes from knowing that Christ's work guarantees the goal of our salvation. Nothing is greater than this. The Holy Spirit uses the time we spend in God's Word, corporate worship, and the Sacrament to prepare our hearts and minds, to fill us with the hope that is based in Jesus Christ alone. We set our hope fully on the grace that will be brought to us at the revelation of Jesus Christ. When our time of testing comes, we have been prepared. We can face the challenges with hope.

Grant it, Lord, that "my hope is built on nothing less" (LSB *575:1). Amen.*

Hope in the Lord

> But this I call to mind, and therefore I have hope: The steadfast love of the LORD never ceases; His mercies never come to an end; they are new every morning; great is Your faithfulness. "The LORD is my portion," says my soul, "therefore I will hope in Him." (Lamentations 3:21–24)

How many challenges are you facing in your life? Do you ever think, *If I can just get over this challenge, things will be better*. But then . . .

In 2022 I experienced some challenges, including four surgeries. Only one was elective, and the last two were the result of my cancer diagnosis. In a local store I found a small plaque with the phrase: "Trust the next chapter because you know the author."

The Scripture passage from Lamentations 3 offers a clear expression of hope and reminds me of the Author of my life, my loving Lord and Savior, Jesus Christ. His steadfast love never ceases. His mercies never come to an end; they are new every morning. Great is His faithfulness!

For me, sometimes it's a matter of focus. When I focus on me, my challenges, and my health issues, I can quickly get into a "poor me" mood. With the help of the Holy Spirit, my focus changes to the Lord, my portion. By His grace alone, I place my hope in Him.

Where is your focus as you face the challenges of each day? Remember that the Lord's mercies are new every morning. Take Him at His Word and hope in Him.

Dear Lord, thank You for the assurance of Your steadfast love that never ceases, Your mercies that are new every morning, and Your great faithfulness. You are my portion. I will hope in You! In Your name I pray. Amen.

Patient Hope

> Now hope that is seen is not hope. For who hopes for what he sees? But if we hope for what we do not see, we wait for it with patience. (Romans 8:24–25)

My husband has a voice issue that makes talking very difficult, and at times it's impossible for others to understand him. A challenge for anyone to endure—and even more so in his call to serve the church as an ordained pastor. He was not able to preach, teach Bible classes, do counseling, make hospital calls, or visit the homebound. It was devastating and hard for his congregation, and all of us who love him dearly.

In John 5, we read the account of Jesus healing an invalid at the pool of Bethesda. The man had been paralyzed for thirty-eight years. The obstacles to his healing were overwhelming. Everyone there was waiting to be healed. What were his chances? Yet he came daily and didn't give up hope. You may know the rest of the story. Jesus came and told him, "Get up, take up your bed, and walk" (verse 8).

Notice the crippled man did not come looking for Jesus to heal him. The miracle was not dependent on what the man did, or how faithful he was, or even how he pleaded. The healing took place solely because of the mercy of God.

Sometimes we are told we must do more, pray more, trust more, hope more. But this miracle of Jesus reminds us that it is not we who must do more, because He has done all that we need *for us*.

As you and I struggle with situations in life, we struggle not as those who have no hope. Our hope is in Jesus alone, and we wait with patience.

Precious Lord, our hope is in Jesus, who comes to us with Your love, forgiveness, peace, and one day perfect healing. In His name. Amen.

Kay
Kreklau

Daily Hope

For this reason, because I have heard of your faith in the Lord Jesus and your love toward all the saints, I do not cease to give thanks for you, remembering you in my prayers, that the God of our Lord Jesus Christ, the Father of glory, may give you the Spirit of wisdom and of revelation in the knowledge of Him, having the eyes of your hearts enlightened, that you may know what is the hope to which He has called you, what are the riches of His glorious inheritance in the saints, and what is the immeasurable greatness of His power toward us who believe, according to the working of His great might. (Ephesians 1:15–19)

It was a stormy night in North Dakota. The weather quickly turned into a blizzard. If you've ever traveled the roads of North Dakota, you will know how treacherous such a night can be. Mark and I were driving home on a paved but untraveled road. The blizzard had reduced visibility to just inches in front of the car. With our windows down so we could look out and search for the edge of the pavement, we crept along.

A few miles away, Aunt Amanda was at home and had noticed the storm. She turned off the television. And without distraction, she prayed for our safety.

Suddenly, as we drove, the path ahead of us cleared.

The storm still swirled around us but the road ahead of us cleared a few feet at a time until we slowly—safely—reached our destination. We didn't know at the time that we were covered by Aunt Amanda's prayers, and she did not know the strength of the storm, she just prayed for God to protect and guide us. I believe we made it home because of her fervent, faithful words on our behalf.

Sometimes, we pray without knowing the details of the circumstances. We don't have to know them—because God does.

I suggest that you write Ephesians 1:17–19, on an index card or in your prayer journal. Memorize the words. And daily pray them for yourself and for your loved ones. Be bold in your prayers in Jesus' name and know that God hears them.

To Him be the Glory!

Lord God, our refuge and shield, guide and protect us today and everyday as we go about the work You have set before us to do in Your name. We thank You for faithful people like Aunt Amanda, who are confident in their prayers to You. In Jesus' name. Amen.

Hope and Promise

> If in Christ we have hope in this life only, we are of all people most to be pitied. But in fact Christ has been raised from the dead, the firstfruits of those who have fallen asleep. For as by a man came death, by a man has come also the resurrection of the dead. For as in Adam all die, so also in Christ shall all be made alive. (1 Corinthians 15:19–22)

What is your hope? What is the Christian hope? In this life we will have problems, trials, and tribulations, which are often considered failures to the world. Looking at those same problems through the eyes of the Christian, we know they are all temporary. We know Christ is coming again, and there will be dancing and leaping and singing! In Christ, joy will be for everyone! Imagine the physically disabled, the deaf, and the blind! Imagine seeing everything in every color in the spectrum of light after a lifetime of darkness. Imagine hearing and singing praises to our Lord after never knowing the sweet sound of a mother's voice or the singing of the doxology. We will be with our Lord, and we will be made perfect! How do we know this? Jesus promises:

> I am the resurrection and the life. Whoever believes in Me, though he die, yet shall he live. (John 11:25)

In our earthly life, all the problems, all the trials, all the tribulations, all the seeming failures are looked at by Christians through the lens of Christ's coming again at the end of the world. While we may experience these things, these sufferings, in Christ we have the hope and promise of eternal life. What a comfort!

Heavenly Father, thank You for the gift of eternal life. Let me always remember the hope that comes only through You! In Jesus' name. Amen.

Addison Grace

> And again, "Praise the Lord, all you Gentiles, and let all the peoples extol Him." And again Isaiah says, "The root of Jesse will come, even He who arises to rule the Gentiles; in Him will the Gentiles hope." May the God of hope fill you with all joy and peace in believing, so that by the power of the Holy Spirit you may abound in hope. (Romans 15:11–13)

The early morning phone call woke us and came with shocking news. During the wee hours of the morning, our granddaughter had died shortly after she was born. Our lives were shattered. We had been so excited to cuddle this new little person, but God had instead welcomed Addison Grace into His loving arms.

As we drove to be with our son and daughter-in-law, we drove in silence, stunned and wondering why. After all the years of praying and waiting for this baby, why had God taken her away? We knew she was a child of God's. His child from conception. But the grief was real for our family.

> Be still before the Lord and wait patiently for Him. (Psalm 37:7)

God's Word reminded us of His hope and faithfulness. Be still. Don't try figure out this world; let God's Word fill your being with comfort and guidance.

> May the God of hope fill you with all joy and peace in believing, so that by the power of the Holy Spirit you may abound in hope. (Romans 15:13)

Through God's Word, we did receive the hope that moved us beyond our days of grief. I encourage you to immerse yourself in His Word and prayer at all times and in all circumstances. Rejoice in God's will for your lives! Trust that He hears your prayers, loves you unconditionally, and draws you to His promise of forgiveness, grace, and salvation in Jesus.

> *Dear Jesus, keep us close to You today and always. Send Your Spirit to comfort those who grieve. Strengthen our faith, knowing that one day we will be with You in heaven. Amen.*

The Big C

> Now may our Lord Jesus Christ Himself, and God our Father, who loved us and gave us eternal comfort and good hope through grace, comfort your hearts and establish them in every good work and word. (2 Thessalonians 2:16–17)

The word *cancer* seemed to scream at me as I drove home from the doctor's office that afternoon. How would I tell my children that I have cancer? What did all of this mean? And then the words of 2 Thessalonians reminded me that God has everything under control.

These words assured me that we have a God who loves us dearly and is always with us. He gives us hope and comfort through His grace, given to us without limit or condition through Jesus dying on the cross for us.

Even as I struggled with the shock and uncertainty of my diagnosis, I was confident God would be with me and my family in the scary days ahead. He would comfort and strengthen me. God would calm my fears and the fears of my family; we only needed to trust and stand firm in Him.

As Paul prayed this blessing over the Thessalonians, I also pray for each of you: May the God of all comfort be with each of you in the midst of all heartaches and challenges. May you know His hope through His grace each day. May you be strengthened in every good work and word as you grow in His saving faith.

Hear us, Jesus. Amen.

Running Behind

> And we desire each one of you to show the same earnestness to have the full assurance of hope until the end, so that you may not be sluggish, but imitators of those who through faith and patience inherit the promises. (Hebrews 6:11–12)

I woke up late. So late that I had no time for my morning devotions. With feelings of regret, I started my day a little frazzled because I had to rush, and a little sluggish because I couldn't follow my daily routine. All day, I knew I had missed something, a big something. That's because my time in His Word is the most important time of my day.

God's Word gives me my marching orders for the day. It inspires me to be patient instead of rude, kind instead of inconsiderate. On the days—and we all have them—when life is just tough, my morning devotions carry me through with knowledge that God works all things to my good according to His will for me. And He *is* with me. I am reminded that Jesus suffered the same things in life that I do—and more. Through the working of the Holy Spirit, I am assured of the continual hope and love we have in Jesus Christ.

Time spent in prayer and in reading the Word of God are where we take our questions, find our comfort, and proclaim our praises. His counsel will always be truthful and for our very best. James 1:5 promises us, "If any of you lacks wisdom, let him ask God, who gives generously to all without reproach, and it will be given him."

My dear friend, however and whenever it works into your daily routine, take time to talk to God and to hear His Word for you in the Bible. Take your questions, concerns, joys, and sorrows to Him in prayer. Receive His Word of forgiveness, love, hope, mercy, and peace. He loves you! He understands you! Be blessed by the Holy Spirit!

We thank and praise You, O God, through Jesus, Your dear Son, that You keep us in Your care. Amen.

Patti
Ross

Assurance

> For I know the plans I have for you, declares the LORD, plans for welfare and not for evil, to give you a future and a hope. (Jeremiah 29:11)

How often have you been present with a mother and her infant child and seen this happen? The mother leaves the room and the infant wails and cries until she appears again. To that infant, when Mom goes into the other room, she is gone. Disappeared. Vanished from the earth. The child is not being dramatic or trying to get mother's attention; he is mourning. Grieving. His mother is no more!

But we know that Mom will be coming back. In fact, she may have left the room to get something to help him, like a diaper or a bottle. Every action she takes is for his welfare. But he doesn't know that, and so he frets.

Sometimes, we are more like babies than adults when we think God has deserted us. We don't feel our prayers are being answered, and we don't feel assured that we will see Him. Jesus reminds His disciples in John 14:2–3:

> In My Father's house are many rooms. If it were not so, would I have told you that I go to prepare a place for you? And if I go

> and prepare a place for you, I will come again and will take you to Myself, that where I am you may be also.

Cradling the child, the mother notes the smile of recognition on the tear-stained face, saying, "Didn't you know I'd come back?" When we have doubts and disappointments, God stands ready to reassure us that He will return and take us to Himself. That is a sure hope.

Our assurance, our hope, is knowing Jesus died for all our sins, rose from the grave, and is readying our "room" in heaven. What a hope! What a future!

Holy Spirit, build our trust in the Lord's presence in our lives, now and forever. In Jesus' name. Amen.

Blessed Hope

> For the grace of God has appeared, bringing salvation for all people, training us to renounce ungodliness and worldly passions, and to live self-controlled, upright, and godly lives in the present age, waiting for our blessed hope, the appearing of the glory of our great God and Savior Jesus Christ. (Titus 2:11–13)

One of the churches I belonged to years ago used an evangelism program that included calling on people and asking them, "If you die tonight, will you go to heaven?" Some would call that an aggressive approach, but it brought some answers that we might expect: "Well, I hope I do," and "Well, I like to think I've been good enough."

We often use the word *hope* to express uncertainty, as the person did when he said he hoped he was going to heaven. But the hope of the Bible is not just a wish for something to happen or a desire for something good in the future. Biblical hope is a confident expectation. The assurance that Jesus died for our sins and rose from the grave. Because of His works, not ours, we will spend eternity in heaven with Him.

Paul speaks of it as "blessed hope," the appearing of the glory of our great God and Savior, Jesus Christ. He urges us as we wait in this present day to live godly lives, but unlike the second respondent, not in order to earn heaven but to glorify God and to love our neighbors as He commanded.

When asked the question "If you die tonight, will you go to heaven?" answer confidently, "That is my blessed hope."

Holy Spirit, help me to share my blessed hope with people you put in my path. In Jesus' name. Amen.

Praise the Lord

> Blessed is he whose help is the God of Jacob, whose hope is in the LORD his God, who made heaven and earth, the sea, and all that is in them, who keeps faith forever; who executes justice for the oppressed, who gives food to the hungry. The LORD sets the prisoners free; the LORD opens the eyes of the blind. The LORD lifts up those who are bowed down; the LORD loves the righteous. The LORD watches over the sojourners; He upholds the widow and the fatherless, but the way of the wicked He brings to ruin. The LORD will reign forever, your God, O Zion, to all generations. Praise the LORD! (Psalm 146:5–10)

Our hope is an assurance that we will be with our God in eternity. And what a great God we have! He gives us that hope as a gift through His grace (2 Thessalonians 2:16). Through Christ's death and resurrection, when He took on our sin and overcame death and the devil, we have that hope, that assurance of spending eternity with Him.

This psalm mirrors Isaiah's prophetic words in Isaiah 61. This passage praises God's nature to secure justice and care for His people. We have the example in the incarnate Word, Jesus Christ, who Himself quotes the Old Testament prophet Isaiah and then concludes,

"Today this Scripture has been fulfilled in your hearing" (Luke 4:17–21).

It's a good psalm to read when you are experiencing hardships or disappointments in this life. It assures us that God is watching over us and that He sees all manner of injustice that we experience. He provides what we need. He is in charge. And He will be in charge forever, to all generations. We may not always see that, but our hope is in the Lord our God. That hope keeps us going through good times and bad.

With the psalmist we sing,

> *Praise You, Lord God, for Your gift of grace and hope for eternity. In Jesus' name and for His sake. Amen.*

Rejoicing and Working

Let love be genuine. Abhor what is evil; hold fast to what is good. Love one another with brotherly affection. Outdo one another in showing honor. Do not be slothful in zeal, be fervent in spirit, serve the Lord. Rejoice in hope, be patient in tribulation, be constant in prayer. Contribute to the needs of the saints and seek to show hospitality. (Romans 12:9–13)

The son we haven't seen for eight months is coming home for a visit! We are rejoicing! We are happy! We are cleaning his room, cooking favorite meals, staying up late to drive to the airport. We are doing usual things with unusually cheerful energy! We have a confident expectation for something good in the future—our reunification with our son.

In and through Jesus, we have a hope, a certainty, and a confidence that something good will happen. And that is our eternal life in heaven, which, by the grace of God, Jesus Christ achieved for us by His death on the cross and the resurrection from the grave. We certainly rejoice in that certainty!

And because we rejoice over this hope, we gladly go about doing tasks that Paul starts to list in these verses. We do our work with love. Just look at the list in chapter

12, and certain words really jump out: *genuine love*, *hold fast*, *show honor*, *be zealous*, *fervent*, *pray*, *contribute*, *show hospitality*, and more in verses 14–21.

Hope stimulates good works!

In our sinful nature, we are unable to do all this perfectly, but the Holy Spirit will help us in our weakness. Jesus is coming—that's our certain hope. While we wait, we do His work energetically and cheerfully.

Our son was happy to see us. Jesus is coming and will be happy to see us too! That's a certainty we rejoice in!

Lord, I rejoice in the hope You have given me. Help me to humbly and joyfully use the gifts You've given me to serve others. Amen.

Our Anchor

> So when God desired to show more convincingly to the heirs of the promise the unchangeable character of His purpose, He guaranteed it with an oath, so that by two unchangeable things, in which it is impossible for God to lie, we who have fled for refuge might have strong encouragement to hold fast to the hope set before us. We have this as a sure and steadfast anchor of the soul, a hope that enters into the inner place behind the curtain, where Jesus has gone. (Hebrews 6:17–20)

It was a beautiful day with calm seas. We headed out with family and friends on the boat to dive and see the vibrant underwater creations of God. Reaching the dive site, we anchored near a reef. The divers geared up, entered the water, and enjoyed a great dive until it was time to return to the boat. Due to heavy rains the day before, a heavy amount of fresh water draining off the island was mixing with the salt water in the sandy area we had to traverse to return to the boat. It caused a deadly current, roiling the sand to where visibility was very poor. Swimming perpendicular with the heavy current, we made progress by reaching and holding on to small rock formations in the sand. We reached the security of the mooring line and grasped the rope that attached the boat to the anchor. Holding on to the rope, we went through our safety steps and boarded the boat, exhausted and relieved.

It's a true event that I often think of when I think of hope being the anchor of the soul. We faced the possibility of death by being swept out to sea. Our rope (anchor) was there to hold on to. We did not make the rope or put it there. It was a sure thing put there for us to grab on to for safety.

We do nothing to deserve the hope we have in Jesus. By the promised grace of God, Jesus Christ saves us from eternal death. His suffering on the cross and His resurrection enable us to grab and hold on to the hope anchoring our soul. This hope, as an anchor, holds us steady in this earthly life and secure in our heavenly future because it is firmly attached to the eternal throne of God.

When we are unsure, doubtful, or scared, Holy Spirit, remind us of the hope that anchors our soul. In Jesus' name. Amen.

Debbie
Larson

Hope in the Lord

I wait for the Lord, my soul waits, and in His word I hope; my soul waits for the Lord more than watchmen for the morning, more than watchmen for the morning. O Israel, hope in the Lord! For with the Lord there is steadfast love, and with Him is plentiful redemption. (Psalm 130:5–7)

A dear friend was diagnosed with ovarian cancer. She was whisked off to surgery, and I waited for news from her husband. My prayers began to flow for her, her family, the medical staff, and for Jesus to calm my anxious heart.

> Do not be anxious about anything, but in everything by prayer and supplication with thanksgiving let your requests be made known to God. And the peace of God, which surpasses all understanding, will guard your hearts and your minds in Christ Jesus. (Philippians 4:6–7)

Waiting is a challenge for many of us. Technology boasts the capability to provide immediate answers, but only our Savior can provide the peace that comes from faith through grace. Waiting on the Lord does not mean waiting for Him to appear. God is always with us! Waiting on the Lord means trusting Him, His timing, and His love.

As I waited for news of a successful surgery, I prayed. I know God answers my prayers in His time and in His way for our good. I know He hears, I trust in His mercy, and I find peace.

How blessed we are to wait with certain hope!

Father, as my soul waits for You, I feel anxious thoughts melt away. Your peace fills my heart. With You, Lord, there is steadfast love and redemption, and I rejoice in the hope You provide. I am filled with thanksgiving as I praise You. In Jesus' name and for His sake. Amen.

In Hope of Eternal Life

> Paul, a servant of God and an apostle of Jesus Christ, for the sake of the faith of God's elect and their knowledge of the truth, which accords with godliness, in hope of eternal life, which God, who never lies, promised before the ages began and at the proper time manifested in His word through the preaching with which I have been entrusted by the command of God our Savior. (Titus 1:1–3)

In Paul's letter to Titus, he reinforces his relationship with Jesus and his reason for sharing the Gospel. He asked Titus to preach the truth to God's children so they would live in the Lord's grace and be saved. Titus was to emphasize that we are justified by God's grace alone, not by our own works.

You and I have a relationship with Jesus, and we have every reason to share the Gospel message. Christ has saved us from our sins, and He offers us peace and strength in difficult times. He has also equipped us to share our faith. Jesus sets a perfect example for us through His actions and teachings. He provides for our joy now and a certain hope for eternal life in heaven. This is Good News to proclaim!

God wants all people to share in His grace and mercy, and we are directed to make disciples of all nations. Let's thank Jesus for His saving grace and ask Him to give us the courage to share His love wherever we go.

Father, I'm humbled and thankful that You revealed to me the message and hope of eternal life. I ask that You put situations in my path that will allow me to share Jesus and His message of salvation with everyone. In Jesus' name. Amen.

Hope in Christ Revealed

> To make the word of God fully known, the mystery hidden for ages and generations but now revealed to His saints. To them God chose to make known how great among the Gentiles are the riches of the glory of this mystery, which is Christ in you, the hope of glory. (Colossians 1:25–27)

I heard this anecdote as a child. As you worship in your church, you may delight in the stained-glass windows as the sun causes rainbows to dance across the pews. The beauty of the glass and in each rainbow is exquisite! Outside the church, those that pass by the building see only darkened windows because the sun is not illuminating the windows from the outsider's point of view. You must be inside the church to see the effect of the sunshine through the stained glass.

To see the glory of God's promises and feel the peace of His forgiveness, we must know Jesus. God shares our need for a Savior, His promise of salvation, and His will for our lives through the Bible. The more we read and understand Scripture, the better we know Jesus.

God desires all people to be saved and come to the knowledge of the truth. What a privilege we are given to share the Good News! Invite everyone into the family of believers. Through Christian fellowship and the study of His Word, the Holy Spirit will move in their hearts. Allow others to have the beauty of the rainbow, the joy of knowing Jesus, and the pot of gold—the hope of eternal glory!

Jesus, You have revealed the joy of Your salvation to me and given me the honor of telling others of Your great love. I praise and thank You for this privilege. Amen.

Grace and Truth from Christ

> And the Word became flesh and dwelt among us, and we have seen His glory, glory as of the only Son from the Father, full of grace and truth. . . . For from His fullness we have all received, grace upon grace. For the law was given through Moses; grace and truth came through Jesus Christ. (John 1:14, 16–17)

Watching or reading the news has me asking, What is the truth? Did the news anchor just share facts or opinion? Where do I go if I want the complete truth? And if I know the truth, am I equipped to decide whether it is good or bad? Am I capable of forming appropriate and godly views? When I have questions, I go to the Bible.

> If any of you lacks wisdom, let him ask God, who gives generously to all without reproach, and it will be given him. (James 1:5)

God's Word is given to us, and in the Gospel of John, we are assured that Jesus became the Word in human form. We were given the truth not only in the written Word but also in the flesh!

> Jesus said to him, "I am the way, and the truth, and the life. No one comes to the Father except through Me." (John 14:6)

Our faith is founded not on our own reasoning or beliefs but on the infallible Word of God. As baptized children of God, we can be assured that Christ lives within us. We confidently stand strong on the Rock! Our views should align with His truth. Our lives are guided by His Word. Grace and truth abound!

Father, lead me in Your truth and teach me to follow Your will for my life. You abound in grace and mercy. May all of creation praise the name of Jesus! In His name. Amen.

Hope and Encouragement

> But since we belong to the day, let us be sober, having put on the breastplate of faith and love, and for a helmet the hope of salvation. . . . Therefore encourage one another and build one another up, just as you are doing. (1 Thessalonians 5:8, 11)

When my kids were small and I would catch them doing something they shouldn't, they'd look astonished and ask, "Mom, how did you know?" I would reply, "I'm a mother. I see and know everything." They believed that—for a second or two.

There were times when I wished I had a superpower. If I could see through walls or have super strength, perhaps I would be able to protect my loved ones better.

But I am reminded that I don't need a superpower. I have an all-powerful God! The battle against the evil foe has been won. The victory is ours! That does not mean we won't experience trouble, as sin exists all around us, but Jesus walks with us and God has provided His protection. I have not been given a cape, but I have been given armor—spiritual armor designed by God. Our battles seem to be of this world, but our battles are not against flesh and blood—they are against the deceitful forces of Satan.

Satan tempted Adam and Eve, and he continues to tempt all Christians. Stand strong, wearing the whole armor of God, as in Ephesians 6:10–20. Stand with confidence and encourage one another. We have hope in Christ!

> The LORD is on my side; I will not fear.
> What can man do to me? (Psalm 118:6)

Ask God to search your heart and guide you to encourage others in their walk of faith.

Lord Jesus, thank You for protecting me from the ways of the evil one. Search my heart. Where I have worry and doubt, replace it with hope and confidence in You. Amen.

Eden
Keefe

The Answer Is Always Jesus

For all the promises of God find their Yes in Him. That is why it is through Him that we utter our Amen to God for His glory. (2 Corinthians 1:20)

Have you heard the story of a pastor giving a children's message, talking about a furry animal with a bushy tail that eats nuts? When he asks the children what he is describing, one finally says, "Well, I know the answer is Jesus. But it sure sounds like a squirrel."

The child was correct on both counts. The pastor was describing a squirrel, and the answer is always found in Jesus!

Throughout the Old Testament, God's promises are recorded. They are for the benefit of His children and for His glory. One of my favorites is, "He will swallow up death forever; and the Lord God will wipe away tears from all faces" (Isaiah 25:8). Then, during Jesus' time on earth, His covenant promises are fulfilled. "For all have sinned and fall short of the glory of God, and are justified by His grace as a gift, through the redemption that is in Christ Jesus" (Romans 3:23–24).

That is why we say amen at the end of our prayers and in our liturgy. *Amen* means, "Yes, it is so," or "Let it be so for me." We affirm our trust that God faithfully keeps all His promises and that the answer has always been Jesus.

As you end your personal prayers, consider replacing "amen" with "In Jesus' name. Yes, it is so," or "In Jesus' name, let it be so for me."

What are some of your favorite promise verses? Text or write one out to share with someone who might need some hope-filled encouragement.

Amen, Lord! I praise and thank You that You cover me with grace and fill me with hope. In Jesus' name. Amen!

Fear Not, Chosen One

> But now thus says the Lord, He who created you, O Jacob, He who formed you, O Israel: "Fear not, for I have redeemed you; I have called you by name, you are Mine. When you pass through the waters, I will be with you; and through the rivers, they shall not overwhelm you; when you walk through fire you shall not be burned, and the flame shall not consume you. For I am the Lord your God, the Holy One of Israel, your Savior. (Isaiah 43:1–3)

I know we do not see the word *Trinity* in the Bible, but this word is a beautiful description of our triune God—the great I AM, Creator, Redeemer, Sanctifier—and what He promises to us, His beloved children.

Read again what Yahweh says: "Fear not . . . you are Mine." You are chosen. You are His. Not because of what you have or haven't done. Only because of who He is!

In this knowledge, we can live securely, trusting in our Father's care. We can find comfort and peace because He is with us. Our hope is fully in Him.

Let's pray these verses in a personal way.

Almighty God, Creator, Redeemer, Sanctifier, in Your Word You have declared "fear not," but there are times that I am afraid, anxious, or concerned. As Your chosen, beloved child, I come to You for Your promised protection and care. As I pass through [insert your situation or difficulty], You will be with me. The worries and concerns will not overwhelm me. As I go through this, I will not be consumed. I thank You, almighty God, for Your great love for me, shown especially through Your Son, Jesus, my Savior. Hold me close to You and grant me Your peace. In Jesus' name. Amen.

Where Is Hope in Tragedy?

Christ Jesus our hope. (1 Timothy 1:1)

The book of Job is a somber read. Job suffers tragedy upon tragedy, and for no apparent reason. Friends who come to offer advice do not help the situation. In fact, one friend, Zophar, tells Job that if he will prepare his heart and put his sin away from him, surely then he will be secure and have hope (see Job 11:13–18).

But Job wasn't buying it—and neither should we! On our own, we can't prepare our hearts or put our sins away from us. In fact, the Bible tells us that by nature, we "were dead in [our] trespasses and sins" (Ephesians 2:1). There is no security or hope when we rely on what we can do.

Let's face it—we are not in control. Thanks be to God that He is!

> But God, being rich in mercy, because of the great love with which He loved us, even when we were dead in our trespasses, made us alive together with Christ—by grace you have been saved. (Ephesians 2:4–5)

Our hope and security rest in Him. He is with us. In the good times. In the bad times. Now and through eternity.

Please join me in praying:

Take my will and make it Thine,
It shall be no longer mine;
Take my heart, it is Thine own,
It shall be Thy royal throne.
Take my love, my Lord, I pour
At Thy feet its treasure store;
Take myself, and I will be
Ever, only, all for Thee. (*LSB* 783:5,6)

Rejoice in Hope

> Let love be genuine. . . . Love one another with brotherly affection. . . . Be fervent in spirit, serve the Lord. Rejoice in hope, be patient in tribulation, be constant in prayer. (Romans 12:9–12)

Just as in 1 Corinthians 13, what many people call the "love chapter," we see genuine love described in Romans 12:9–21. Read the entire passage as you have time.

As children of God, we live in God's grace and seek to reflect His love in our lives. Among the list of ways to show Christlike love, we find verse 12: "Rejoice in hope, be patient in tribulation, be constant in prayer."

Let's look at the first imperative, "Rejoice in hope." This is the hope of our salvation, won for us by Christ. It is ours by grace through faith. This hope endures because salvation is ours for eternity.

Knowing that, we can "be patient in tribulation" since tribulation is not ours for eternity! "He will wipe away every tear from their eyes, and death shall be no more, neither shall there be mourning, nor crying, nor pain anymore, for the former things have passed away" (Revelation 21:4).

And knowing God, we can "be constant in prayer" because He always hears and answers. "When the righteous cry for help, the Lord hears and delivers them out of all their troubles" (Psalm 34:17).

Now those are hope-filled reasons to rejoice!

Reflect on the following questions: How is rejoicing in hope shown in my worship and prayers? How is it visible in my daily interactions?

Holy Spirit, fill our lives so that our joy in the sure and certain hope of our salvation flows out of us. May we joyfully proclaim Christ and honor You by serving others. In Jesus' name. Amen.

Jesus Is My Anchor

We who have fled for refuge might have strong encouragement to hold fast to the hope set before us. We have this as a sure and steadfast anchor of the soul. (Hebrews 6:18–19)

Do you remember Cajun chef Justin Wilson, the television personality who had a syndicated cooking show? He often used the catchphrase "I guarantee!" during his shows.

In Hebrews 6:18, we read that God guaranteed His unchangeable character so that "we who have fled for refuge might have strong encouragement to hold fast to the hope set before us." I understand the desire to flee to Him for refuge, but what exactly is the hope set before us? It is Christ's promise that He will return in glory.

> When the Son of Man comes in His glory, and all the angels with Him, then He will sit on His glorious throne. (Matthew 25:31)

It is the promise that by the gift of grace through faith we will share eternal life with our Savior!

> I will come again and will take you to Myself, that where I am you may be also. (John 14:3)

The author of Hebrews goes on to assert that "we have this as a sure and steadfast anchor of the soul" (Hebrews 6:19). So when the ups and downs—the storms of life—feel chaotic and cause anxiety, Christ our anchor holds us securely. We have God's guarantee!

On a note card, sketch an anchor, or find an image and print it out. Write out the verses above or "Jesus is my anchor." Place it where you will see it often and be reminded of this promise.

Heavenly Father, thank You for the guarantee of Your promises. When I feel tossed by the storms of life, hold me securely in my faith. Even then, may my life reflect Your love and grace to others. Anchor my soul in Christ. In Jesus' name. Amen.